CHESTER A.
ARTHUR

PRESIDENTIAL ✦ LEADERS

CHESTER A. ARTHUR

RUTH TENZER FELDMAN

TWENTY-FIRST CENTURY BOOKS/MINNEAPOLIS

To Peg Goldstein for her encouragement, good humor,
and "neatnik"-itude.

Twenty-First Century Books
A division of Lerner Publishing Group
241 First Avenue North
Minneapolis, MN 55401 U.S.A.

Website address: www.lernerbooks.com

Library of Congress Cataloging-in-Publication Data

Feldman, Ruth Tenzer.
    Chester A. Arthur / by Ruth Tenzer Feldman.
        p.   cm. — (Presidential leaders)
    Includes bibliographical references and index.
    ISBN-13: 978–0–8225–1512–8 (lib. bdg. : alk. paper)
    ISBN-10: 0–8225–1512–1 (lib. bdg. : alk. paper)
    1. Arthur, Chester Alan, 1829–1886—Juvenile literature. 2. Presidents—United States—
Biography—Juvenile literature. I. Title. II. Series.
E692.F45   2007
973.8'4092—dc22   2006016444

Manufactured in the United States of America
1 2 3 4 5 6 – JR – 12 11 10 09 08 07

CONTENTS

———— ✧ ————

Chester A. Arthur was president from
September 20, 1881, to March 4, 1885.

INTRODUCTION

The hours of Garfield's life are numbered—
before this meets your eye, you may be President.
—Julia Sand, letter to Chester A. Arthur, August 1881

During the hot sunny days of August 1881, New York City bustled with activity around Chester Alan Arthur's three-story town house at 123 Lexington Avenue. But Arthur rarely stepped outside. His wife had recently died, leaving in his care their two children: Nell, aged nine, and Alan, seventeen. Normally, Arthur would have been traveling the country or giving speeches instead of staying at home with his family. He was, after all, the vice president of the United States.

The president was James Garfield. Garfield was known as an honest, hardworking politician. Chester Arthur, by contrast, was known for throwing elegant dinners, wearing fashionable clothes, and taking part in the corrupt politics of New York City. Although both men were Republicans, they came from opposing factions of the party. Republican leaders had chosen Arthur as Garfield's running mate mostly because they had needed New York's votes to win the presidential election.

A few people worried that Chester Arthur might not be fit for the job of vice president. But some noted that even if he weren't, the vice president rarely played an important role in running the country. One commentator wrote, "[T]here is no place in which the powers will be so small as in the vice presidency."

Only a few months later, the commentator found out how wrong he was. On July 2, 1881, a deranged man, who supported Arthur's faction of Republicans, fired two shots at President Garfield. The shooter believed he had killed Garfield, paving the way for Arthur to take over as president. "Arthur will be President!" the man shouted shortly after he fired his gun. But President Garfield did not die. He clung to life throughout the summer.

Rumors circulated that Chester Arthur had had something to do with the shooting. These rumors deeply upset Arthur. He tried hard to avoid all contact with newspaper reporters and people on the street. He didn't want to become president under such circumstances and didn't want to discuss the situation. He clung to the hope that Garfield would recover.

Toward the end of August, a letter came to the house from someone named Julia Sand. The first few lines echoed what many people seemed to think of Chester Arthur. "The people are bowed in grief," Sand wrote, "but—do you realize it?—not so much because [Garfield] is dying, as because *you* are his successor." In other words, Sand said, Americans were upset that Arthur might become president.

Arthur read further. "Great emergencies awaken generous traits which have lain dormant [sleeping] half a life. If there is a spark of true nobility in you, now is the occasion to let it shine. . . . Faith in your better nature forces me to write to you—but not to beg you to resign. Do what is more difficult & more brave. Reform!" With these words, Sand urged Arthur to give up his corrupt dealings and become a better man.

Arthur did not know anyone named Julia Sand. After some investigation, he learned that the return address on the letter was a house owned by a banker named Theodore V. Sand. Julia might have been Sand's sister, daughter, or wife. Arthur did not know which. What he did know was that Julia Sand was one of the few who had faith in his "better nature"—one of the very, very few.

Meanwhile, Arthur kept the green blinds closed throughout the house, shutting in his children and shutting out anyone who might look in the windows. He waited. And he saved the letter.

CHAPTER ONE

THE PREACHER'S BOY

*What a life we did lead . . . sitting up like
owls till two or three in the morning . . .
quite satisfied with our little world.*
—Chester A. Arthur, recalling his childhood,
December 11, 1850

Chester Alan Arthur was just what his father wanted—a boy! Born on October 5, 1829, the new baby had four sisters ahead of him: Regina, aged seven; Jane, aged five; Almeda, three; and baby Ann, only twenty-two months.

There was barely room for another child in the Arthurs' tiny log cabin in North Fairfield, Vermont. But when Malvina Arthur gave birth to a son, her husband, William, was so happy that he was said to have "danced up and down the room." William named the boy Chester in honor of Chester Abell, a doctor and close friend who had helped with the delivery. Alan, the infant's middle name, was the name of William's father.

William Arthur, Chester's father, was a Baptist minister with a quick temper.

William Arthur was a Baptist minister. He was known by the honorary title Elder Arthur. Shortly after Chester's birth, the family moved to a parsonage, a house that Elder Arthur's congregation had built for them. But Elder Arthur had a quick temper. He sometimes made hurtful remarks to church members during sermons. Because of Elder Arthur's stormy nature, he never stayed with one congregation very long. The family had already moved several times in Canada and Vermont before Chester came along.

The Arthurs stayed in North Fairfield until Chester's fifth sister was born in 1832. Her name was Malvina. Then the family moved again, this time to Williston, Vermont. The next year, the Arthurs moved to Hinesburgh, Vermont. Chester's brother, William, was born there in 1834.

In 1835 the Arthurs moved to Perry, a small town in the western part of New York. Chester's second brother, George, was born there in 1836. About a year later, the

Arthurs moved a few miles east to the town of York, where young George died in 1838.

In addition to his fiery temper, Elder Arthur held strong beliefs on many issues. For instance, he firmly believed that slavery was immoral. He often included this message in his sermons. New York had already outlawed slavery, but some other U.S. states and territories still allowed it. Slavery was widespread in the South. There, wealthy landowners used African American slaves to work their plantations, or large farms.

In fact, Elder Arthur had helped start the New York branch of the American Anti-Slavery Society. This organization was devoted to abolishing (ending) slavery in the United States. It also wanted African Americans to have the same rights that white citizens enjoyed. But many white people disagreed with the abolitionists. Some white people argued that it was up to the citizens of each state to decide whether or not to allow slavery. Others wanted to send former slaves to Africa—the birthplace of their ancestors.

SCHOOL DAYS

In November 1839, the Arthurs moved farther east, to Union Village (modern-day Greenwich), a small town north of Albany, New York. This was the fifth time Chester had changed locations since he was born, not counting the move from the log cabin to the parsonage in North Fairfield. In all this time, Chester did not attend school. He learned the basics of reading and writing from his father at home.

Finally, at the age of ten, Chester stayed put for a few years. His father became the minister at the Bottskill Baptist Church in Union Village. His pay was about $500 (about

$9,000 in modern money) per year. Finally, Chester entered a local school for boys.

Unlike his father, who often angered people, Chet—as he was known by then—had an agreeable, friendly personality. He also liked to take charge. A companion of his in Union Village remembered Chet watching the village boys build a mud dam after a rain shower. After a while, Chet began telling the boys how to build the dam. They followed his instructions without question, even though Chet took care not to get any of the dirt on his hands.

Another sister, Mary, was born in 1841. The next year, Chet's older sister, Jane, died at the age of eighteen. In 1844 the family moved to Schenectady, New York, so Elder Arthur could lead the First Baptist Church there. Chet enrolled in the Lyceum, a boys' high school. He thrived at the school. A teacher at the Lyceum described the new fifteen-year-old pupil: "His eyes were dark and brilliant, and his physical system finely formed. He was frank and open in his manners, and genial in his disposition."

Chet studied a classical curriculum, which involved learning Latin and Greek. He soon became coeditor of the school's newspaper, the *Lyceum Review*.

By then Chet had started to follow politics. He had heard many of his father's strong antislavery sermons, and he agreed with his father on the slavery issue. During the presidential campaign of 1844, Whig Party candidate Henry Clay ran against Democrat James Polk. Chet supported Clay, a former U.S. senator and opponent of slavery.

With fellow Clay supporters, Chet built an "ash pole." They cut an ash tree from a nearby forest and stripped off its branches. Pole contests were popular in 1844. The candidate whose followers could erect the tallest pole (sometimes decorated with a flag at the top) was said to be likely to win the election. (Despite Chet's ash pole, Clay lost the election.)

In September 1845, Chet enrolled in Union College, an all-male school in Schenectady. Because of his coursework at the Lyceum, Chet was allowed to skip his freshman year. He started college as a sophomore. A tall, good-looking young man, with dark brown eyes and brown wavy hair, he joined the Psi Upsilon Fraternity, a social club. He lived on campus with the other students and could not leave without permission.

Chet seemed to prefer parties and socializing with classmates to schoolwork. College authorities fined him for skipping chapel. He also got caught throwing the school bell in the Erie Canal and jumping on and off slow-moving trains.

———————————— ✧ ————————————

Chet attended Union College (below) in Schenectady, New York, from 1845 to 1848.

But Chet also kept up with his classes, which included Latin and Greek. He became president of the college's debating society. Like the other students, he began the school day with breakfast at 6:30 A.M. He finished with a 7:00 P.M. study session. To help with college expenses, he taught children in nearby schools during his winter vacation.

In July 1848, Chester Arthur graduated from college in the top third of his class of about eighty students. Because of his good grades, he was awarded membership in Phi Beta Kappa, an academic fraternity. At graduation he gave a speech titled "The Destiny of Genius." By then an abolitionist like his father, eighteen-year-old Chet had a good idea of the career path he wanted to pursue—politics and law. He also wanted to earn enough money to live a comfortable life.

ZACK TACKLES LAW

Chester Arthur continued teaching children after graduation. He attended law school for several months in Ballston Spa, New York. Then he returned to his family home, which was then in Hoosick, New York. Arthur continued his legal studies at home. (During Arthur's time, law students often read law books on their own. They didn't spend years going to law school.)

One of Arthur's good friends was Allen Campbell, whom Arthur nicknamed John. Campbell had a nickname for Arthur too. It was Zack. In 1850 Campbell fell ill, probably with tuberculosis. "Zack . . . his dearest friend," wrote a series of encouraging, sensitive, and caring letters to him.

Among Elder Arthur's other activities, he preached at a church in North Pownal, Vermont. While he continued to study law, Chester Arthur also worked in North Pownal.

CHESTER ARTHUR STILLMAN

Every student in the North Pownal school had to recite something on examination day to an audience of classmates, teachers, important visitors, and parents. But an eight-year-old named Asa Stillman was too shy and fearful to face the audience. With one day to go before the dreaded examination, Asa stayed after school and met with his principal, Chester Arthur. Asa expected Arthur to punish him. Instead, Arthur spoke to Asa gently. He taught him a simple poem, which Asa recited successfully the next day.

Stillman, who grew up to become a doctor, told the story to a newspaper reporter in 1883, when Arthur was president. Stillman still had the poem Arthur had carefully hand printed for him more than thirty years earlier. He was so impressed with his principal's treatment that he named his first son Chester Arthur Stillman.

He taught classes at a school there and became the school principal in 1851. His pupils found him to be thoughtful and generous.

In 1852 Arthur left North Pownal for a higher-paying position. He earned $35 ($775) a month as principal of a boys' school where his sister Malvina taught. The school was in Cohoes, New York, near Albany. During this time, Arthur tried to save as much money as he could. He was eager to live in New York City, a place teeming with influential politicians and important businesspeople.

The Cohoes school presented quite a challenge for the new principal. The boys in the school's upper grade had a reputation for wildness. Four teachers had quit in the past year. Arthur, who was an imposing six foot two, did not threaten the students. Instead, he tried to win their goodwill and cooperation. Whenever a student acted out, Arthur made him spend the rest of the day, including recess, in the primary grade classroom, sitting among the younger children. The technique proved highly successful in curbing bad behavior.

While working as a principal, Arthur also worked in a New York City law office to prepare to qualify as a lawyer. Erastus Culver, an antislavery friend of Elder Arthur's, was the main partner in the office.

In 1854 Culver's law firm filed official papers stating that Chester Arthur had worked for them for more than one year and that he was of good moral character. Arthur was then admitted to the New York bar, meaning he had a license to practice law in that state. Erastus Culver offered him a permanent, paid position in the firm, which changed its name to Culver, Parker and Arthur. Arthur's teaching days were over.

CHAPTER TWO

MAKING A NAME
IN NEW YORK

*[Arguing cases in court] comes rather hard at
first but it will do me a great deal of good.*
—Chester Arthur, March 1855

By the time Chester Arthur became a lawyer, slavery threatened to tear his nation apart. The month that Arthur got his license to practice law—May 1854—Congress passed the Kansas-Nebraska Act. The act established the territories of Kansas and Nebraska. It also let settlers in those territories decide whether to allow or abolish slavery there. In Kansas, settlers did not agree on slavery. The violence between proslavery and abolitionist forces in Kansas Territory led to the nickname Bleeding Kansas.

Slavery was illegal in New York and many other states. But free African Americans in the United States still did not have the same freedoms as white Americans. For instance, African American men were not allowed to vote (women also could not vote, regardless of race). African Americans were not allowed to mix with whites in many public places. Both Chester Arthur and Erastus Culver opposed discrimination against African Americans.

On July 16, 1854, an African American teacher named Elizabeth Jennings refused to leave a whites-only streetcar on the Third Avenue line in New York City. After the streetcar conductor and a police officer forcibly removed Jennings from the streetcar, African American leaders in the city protested. They hired the law firm of Culver, Parker and Arthur to take the case to the Brooklyn Circuit Court.

Chester Arthur handled the case. He sued the Third Avenue Railroad Company for not allowing African Americans to ride on the same streetcars as whites. When the case went

──────────── ✧ ────────────

Elizabeth Jennings was removed from a streetcar much like the one in this scene of Madison Square in New York City.

to trial early in 1855, Arthur showed the judge a new section of the New York laws that related to common carriers—vehicles used by the public. After hearing Arthur's argument, the judge told the jury that the Third Avenue Railroad Company was responsible for the actions of its streetcar conductors. The judge also ruled that "colored persons [African Americans], if sober, well-behaved, and free from disease" could not be forced off streetcars and other types of public transportation.

Thanks to Arthur's work, Jennings won her case. She had sued the company for five hundred dollars. She won half that amount, including the cost of her attorney fees. For years afterward, the Colored Peoples' Legal Rights Association celebrated the anniversary of the Jennings verdict—February 22, 1855.

Peter Porter, an African American man, was refused service on the Eighth Avenue streetcar line a few weeks later. Encouraged by Arthur's success with the Jennings case,

A HUNDRED-YEAR STRUGGLE

Elizabeth Jennings won her case against the Third Avenue Railroad Company on February 22, 1855. But discrimination against African Americans continued in public transportation for another hundred years. On December 1, 1955—a century after the Jennings case in New York City—an African American woman named Rosa Parks refused to give up her seat on a bus to a white passenger in Montgomery, Alabama. Parks was arrested. The African American community in Montgomery staged a year-long boycott against the bus company. The boycott helped end segregation (the separation of races) on the buses there.

Porter sued the streetcar company. He and the owners of the company settled the case without going to court. Soon afterward, all streetcar companies in New York City ended their discrimination against African American riders.

Arthur helped Culver with another important equal rights case. An African American man named Louis Napoleon had asked New York judge Elijah Paine to free a man, two women, and five children. Napoleon claimed that Jonathan Lemmon was holding the group as slaves at a house in New York City. Lemmon explained that he and his wife, Juliet, were citizens of Virginia, a state where slavery was allowed. They and their eight slaves were traveling by steamship to Texas, another slave state, and had to stay for a time in New York.

Using a legal document called a writ of habeas corpus, Judge Paine told Lemmon to hand over the eight individuals. The judge said that New York law made free "every person formerly held as a slave who is introduced into this State by the voluntary act or consent of his master."

The judge's decision caused a storm of outrage among slaveholders. Slaves were considered property. Even those who opposed slavery wondered aloud if the U.S. Constitution gave one state the right to take away the property allowed to a citizen of another state. The legislature of Virginia argued that the judge was wrong. But New York held its ground. Virginia decided to appeal the judge's decision and take the case to a higher court—the New York Supreme Court.

The New York legislature hired Erastus Culver to argue on behalf of the newly freed slaves. Culver brought Arthur into the case. Culver had begun his term as a judge in Brooklyn that year, so Arthur took over most of Culver's work at the law firm. Many months passed before the case came to court.

THE NEW REPUBLICAN PARTY

In 1854 a series of antislavery meetings took place throughout the North. One of the first was held in Ripon, Wisconsin. There, about fifty people met in Ripon's tiny schoolhouse and declared themselves to be antislavery "republicans" (people who vote for government representatives). Erastus Culver and Chester Arthur attended a similar meeting in Saratoga Springs, New York, in the summer of 1854. These meetings led to the creation of the Republican Party.

⸻ ✧ ⸻

The schoolhouse in Ripon (below) *where the Republican Party had its first meeting can still be visited.*

Meanwhile, Arthur devoted much of his time to his new career. He shared a room in a fashionable boarding-house, the Bancroft House, with another young lawyer named Henry Gardiner. He went to the theater from time to time. Arthur worked hard and only occasionally visited with young women.

Arthur made a name for himself as a respected lawyer, particularly for his work on the Jennings and Lemmon cases. In 1856 he and Gardiner opened their own law firm.

STEPPING INTO POLITICS

Arthur also became interested in New York State politics, which was then under the control of Thurlow Weed. A journalist and businessman with extensive connections in the former Whig Party (which had broken up around 1854), Weed was known in New York as the Dictator.

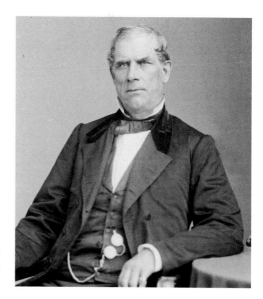

————————————— ✧
Thurlow Weed (right)
dominated New York
State politics from the late
1820s to the 1860s.

Weed was corrupt. To retain power in the state, his workers sometimes bought votes and prevented some people from voting. They sometimes stuffed ballot boxes with fake ballots and "lost" ballot boxes—all to win elections for Weed and his friends.

Weed also handed out government jobs to his supporters. These new jobholders were expected to give part of their salaries to Weed. This form of political activity was part of the spoils system, named for the common slogan "to the victor go the spoils." Weed's system worked so much like well-running machinery that it was called machine politics.

By then the Republican Party had formed. It included many former members of the Whig Party and others who opposed slavery. Chester Arthur supported the new party. In 1856 he campaigned for John Frémont, the Republicans' first candidate for president. He worked at a polling (voting) place at Broadway and Twenty-third Street in New York City. He also joined political committees. But to succeed in New York politics, twenty-seven-year-old Chester Arthur needed to learn to get along with sixty-year-old Thurlow Weed.

Charming and handsome, Arthur dressed fashionably and wore his hair in the current style—just down to his earlobes. But politics and law consumed much of his time. He put little effort into attracting and establishing a serious relationship with a woman. Arthur once wrote to his sister Ann that "I am yet heart-whole."

Then Arthur met Ellen Lewis Herndon. She was a cousin of one of Arthur's good friends, Dabney Herndon. She had come up from Washington, D.C., with her mother to visit Herndon in New York. Nicknamed Nell, she was a

Ellen Herndon was from an influential family in Virginia. She met Arthur through her cousin Dabney Herndon.

——————————— ✧

small, frail, nineteen-year-old. She had dark brown hair, delicate features, and an exceptionally beautiful singing voice. Her parents were influential Virginians. Her father was William Lewis Herndon, a former navy captain noted for his explorations of the Amazon River in South America. Her mother was Frances Elizabeth Hansbrough, well known in Washington society.

Dabney Herndon lived at Bancroft House and often dined with Arthur and Arthur's law partner, Henry Gardiner. He introduced Chet to Nell, and the couple soon developed a close relationship. In 1856 they each spent the summer in the fashionable resort town of Saratoga, New York, overlooking Lake George. There, they fell in love and decided to marry.

Later that year, Arthur and Gardiner headed to Kansas. They wanted to learn more about the situation there and the antislavery movement. On the way, the two men spent time in Wisconsin, Nebraska, and Missouri. They traveled widely in Kansas Territory. Arthur bought land in Leavenworth, Kansas, with the idea of selling it later at a profit. Arthur also attended political rallies, spoke with sheriffs, and interviewed the governor of the territory. He witnessed the violence and hatred between proslavery and antislavery factions. He also saw the general lawlessness in the area. During the trip, he missed Nell deeply and wrote her love letters.

While he was in Kansas Territory, Chester received a letter from Nell asking him to come home. She wrote that her father had drowned on September 12. His steamship, *Central America*, had sunk in a storm off Cape Hatteras, North Carolina. Nell needed Chester's help with the family's financial matters.

Arthur and Gardiner traveled back to New York and resumed their law practice. The slavery case of *Lemmon v. People* finally came before the New York Supreme Court in December 1857. That court decided that Judge Paine had been right to order the Lemmons to give up their eight slaves. This decision further divided proslavery and antislavery forces. Virginia once again rejected the ruling. It took the case to the highest court in New York, the state's Court of Appeals.

On February 3, 1858, Chester Arthur joined the New York State militia, an armed force of ordinary citizens under control of the state governor. The militia worked during state ceremonies and emergencies. Arthur became a judge advocate, or military lawyer, in the militia's Second Brigade. He had no intention of fighting, however. New attorneys often joined the militia as a way to meet political and business leaders, and Arthur aimed to succeed in New York politics.

A MARRIAGE OF NORTH AND SOUTH

Later in February, Arthur took his first trip to the South so he could be with his bride to be. Born in Culpeper Court House, Virginia, Ellen Herndon was an only child. But she had plenty of relatives for Chet Arthur to meet. He spent two weeks in Fredericksburg, Virginia, where he met the Herndon and Hansbrough clans. A family slave attended to Nell and her mother in Fredericksburg.

Arthur presented himself to Dr. Brodie Herndon, who was Nell's uncle and the father of Arthur's friend Dabney Herndon. From all accounts, Arthur made a favorable impression, and it is likely he kept his antislavery opinions to himself. "He is a fine looking man," Dr. Herndon wrote in his diary shortly after he met Arthur, "and we all like him very much."

Arthur returned to New York and continued his advance in the Republican Party. He supported Edwin Morgan, a wealthy New York businessman and a close ally of the

Edwin Morgan got the 1858 nomination to run for governor of New York. He won and served from 1859 to 1862.

party's machine leader, Thurlow Weed. Weed called in favors and used his influence to make sure that Morgan got the Republican nomination for governor of New York in 1858. After Morgan won the election, Arthur took an unpaid position as part of Morgan's personal honor guard—soldiers who appear at ceremonies. In this job, Arthur wore a military uniform and attended to the governor on official occasions.

Chester Alan Arthur and Ellen Lewis Herndon were married on October 25, 1859, in New York City's Calvary Episcopal Church. Nell's widowed mother owned a house at 34 West Twenty-first Street, and the couple moved in with her there.

The Lemmon case came up again in March 1860—this time in the New York Court of Appeals. Again, the higher court ruled that the lower court's decision had been correct. Unhappy with the ruling, Virginia lawyers prepared to argue against the New York decision before the justices of the U.S. Supreme Court.

Meanwhile, Chet and Nell held elaborate dinner parties and entertained influential Republicans in their home. Arthur doted on his new wife, buying her jewelry and clothes. She was a gracious hostess. Soon she and her mother were welcomed into New York's high society.

The Republicans held their second national convention, this time in May 1860 in Chicago. Arthur supported New York senator and former governor William Seward. But the convention chose Abraham Lincoln as its presidential candidate. Maine senator Hannibal Hamlin was Lincoln's running mate. Governor Morgan served as chairman of the Republican National Committee. He worked with Lincoln on fund-raising strategies for the campaign.

By the fall of 1860, Ellen was pregnant. She cut back on her social engagements. At the same time, Arthur actively campaigned for Lincoln, who defeated Democrat Stephen Douglas in November 1860.

Lincoln's election angered many people in the South. Some southern states had threatened to secede (withdraw) from the United States if the antislavery Republicans won the election.

In the Arthur household, William Lewis Herndon Arthur was born on December 10, 1860. He was named for his maternal grandfather. His father was the son of an ardent abolitionist from the North. His mother was a southern belle in a family that owned slaves. Ten days after William was born, South Carolina became the first state to secede from the Union (the United States).

*The Confederate attack on Fort Sumter, South Carolina,
a fort near the entrance to Charleston Harbor, was the first battle
of the Civil War (1861–1865).*

CHAPTER THREE

HELPING THE UNION

During the first two years of the Rebellion
[Chester Arthur] was my chief reliance
in the duties of equipping and transporting
troops and munitions of war.

—Edwin Morgan, governor of New York,
December 1, 1871

By January 1861, the Union was falling apart. That month Alabama, Florida, Georgia, Louisiana, and Mississippi joined South Carolina in seceding from the United States. Delegates from the six states met in February 1861. They formed a government called the Confederate States of America. In March, Texas joined the Confederacy.

On April 12, Confederate soldiers attacked Fort Sumter, a federal (U.S. government) fort in South Carolina. The fort's defenders soon surrendered, and President Lincoln sent Union troops to regain the fort. The Civil War had begun. Virginia, Arkansas, North Carolina, and Tennessee quickly joined the Confederacy.

Chester Arthur and his family felt the conflict keenly. Arthur's mother-in-law believed in the right of states to determine whether or not to allow slavery. She sympathized with the South and no longer felt welcome in the North. So she left the New York City town house she shared with Chet and Ellen and returned to her family in Virginia shortly after the war began.

MORGAN'S MAIN MAN

President Lincoln asked Edwin Morgan and other Union governors to provide soldiers to defeat the Confederate rebellion. The New York legislature voted to spend $5 million for the defense of the state and $3 million to arm and equip thirty thousand volunteer soldiers.

Arthur was called to active duty in the New York State militia. He became engineer in chief for Governor Morgan and held the rank of brigadier general. As engineer in chief, his job was to help the state's quartermaster (supply) office provide clothing, equipment, food, and housing for New York soldiers. Arthur also had to find housing for soldiers from other state militias who gathered in New York City on their way to join the Union army. It was a challenging task. Arthur took it on eagerly and was paid well. In April the governor named him acting assistant quartermaster general.

Since Arthur was officially part of the war effort on the side of the North, he, Nell, and baby William moved to a hotel near Twenty-second Street and Broadway. It didn't seem right to stay in the house owned by Nell's mother, who supported the Confederate South.

As part of his work with the New York State militia, Arthur helped find housing for soldiers from New York and other states. Once in the field, soldiers often slept in tents (right).

────────────── ✧

In the summer of 1861, thousands upon thousands of New Yorkers enlisted in the Union army. Flags flew everywhere, as families gathered to sing patriotic songs and see off the new soldiers to do battle with the Confederacy. Many thought the rebellion would last only a few months.

Arthur worked long hours in a large military warehouse at 51 Walker Street. Governor Morgan slept only a few hours each night and expected his staff to do the same. He demanded that Arthur and other officers do their jobs effectively, efficiently, and fairly.

Arthur took his job very seriously and carried out his duties extremely well. As part of his job, Arthur advised Governor Morgan on military matters. The two men went to Washington, D.C., several times to meet with federal officials. Morgan also sent Arthur to Albany, the New York state capital, to speak with state government officials.

Another aspect of Arthur's job was to inspect forts and other defenses throughout New York State. In January 1862, he drafted a detailed document of the state's defense plans in case of attack by Confederate forces. Newspapers praised Arthur for the thoroughness of the plan. On February 10, Governor Morgan appointed him inspector general of the state militia. In this job, Arthur made sure that everything related to the state militia ran properly and that all state defenses were in good order.

FAMILY FEUD

The war, which many had thought would last only a few months, dragged on with no end in sight. Soldiers and citizens alike endured many hardships. But Governor Morgan paid Chester Arthur very well. He and his family lived quite comfortably during the war. Nell entertained elegantly in the hotel's plush rooms. She was friendly and seemed eager to please her guests in New York. But friends noticed increasing tensions between Arthur and his "little rebel wife," as he jokingly called her.

At the same time, Nell's family members were appalled that her husband was a general in Lincoln's army. Some of her close relatives, including her cousin Dabney Herndon, had joined the Confederate cause. In the course of battle, Union soldiers captured Dabney and eventually sent him to a prison camp on Davids Island in New York City's harbor. Chester arranged for Nell to visit her cousin there several times.

In the spring of 1862, Arthur traveled to Fredericksburg, Virginia. The official reason was to inspect New York troops stationed there. More likely, Arthur's main motive was to visit Nell's family and ensure their safety. He stayed in the South until Governor Morgan ordered him home in June.

The governor promoted him to quartermaster general on July 10. Arthur continued to equip troops and send men to the front. He saw to it that thousands of new recruits were housed, trained, and given arms and uniforms. As a cost-saving measure, he arranged for soldiers, rather than hired laborers, to build two hundred temporary barracks. Thanks in part to Arthur's efforts, 219,000 New Yorkers had enlisted in the Union army and had left for the front by November 1862.

A Union recruiter stands outside Castle Garden,
the New York immigration center, trying to convince
new immigrants to join the Union army.

BILLY WILSON'S WAR

When Billy Wilson decided to take advantage of his neighbors during the Civil War, he didn't count on meeting Chester Arthur. Wilson was a city council member who represented one of the most crime-ridden sections of New York City. He and his buddies dressed in military uniforms and called themselves Union soldiers. They demanded free food from local restaurants and bullied residents into giving them other services. One day General Arthur invited Wilson to his office. Wilson showed up wearing a colonel's uniform and claiming he was in the U.S. Army. Arthur ripped the officer stripes from Wilson's uniform and had him arrested.

Governor Morgan decided not to run for reelection when his term was up in 1862. He later praised Arthur's performance in the militia. "In the position of Quarter Master General he displayed not only great executive ability and unbending integrity, but great knowledge of Army Regulation."

CONKLING AND A CAREER

Democrats won many New York offices in 1862, including the governorship. Since the new governor was expected to give jobs to his own loyal supporters, Arthur knew that he would probably lose his position as quartermaster general. His term of duty with the New York State militia would soon be over anyway. So on January 1, 1863, when the new governor, Horatio Seymour, took office, General

Arthur resigned his post. On the same day, President Lincoln issued the Emancipation Proclamation, a document freeing all slaves in the Confederacy.

Arthur returned to his law practice with Henry Gardiner. He concentrated on earning enough money to pay for the fine lifestyle he had gotten used to on his high military salary. He maintained his contacts with Thurlow Weed and other influential New York Republicans. Among them was Roscoe Conkling. This prominent politician had been mayor of Utica, New York, and then served in the U.S. House of Representatives until his defeat in the 1862 election.

Conkling and Arthur lived near each other in New York City. The two men made a striking pair. Both men were more than six feet tall, stylish dressers, eloquent speakers, and almost exactly the same age. Conkling had been born on October 30,

─────── ✧
Roscoe Conkling (right) *was also a New York lawyer, just like Arthur.*

1829—only twenty-five days after Arthur. There were differences too. Arthur made friends easily and avoided making enemies. Conkling had a hot temper and was quick to take offense.

Conkling held a grudge against James G. Blaine, a Republican congressman from Maine. Conkling claimed that Blaine had insulted him in front of fellow congressmen. But Blaine was not a man to be bullied. He was determined to

James G. Blaine

——— ✧ ———

lead the Republican Party, and he tried to limit Conkling's power. Caught in the conflict and eager to rise in New York politics, Chester Arthur aligned himself with Conkling.

The conflict between the Union and the Confederacy continued. Both sides had victories and defeats. In one battle, the second Battle of Fredericksburg in May 1863, the Herndons' Virginia home was damaged. At about that time, Union general Ulysses Grant won several major battles around Vicksburg, Mississippi. Shortly afterward, Union forces took control over the entire Mississippi River. This move split the Confederate forces in two.

Tragedy struck the Arthurs on July 8, 1863. Chet, Nell, and William were vacationing in Englewood, New Jersey.

During the trip, William got sick, most likely with meningitis, and died. He was only two and a half years old. Arthur and his wife were devastated.

"We have lost our darling boy," Arthur wrote to his brother the next day. "He died . . . from convulsions, brought on by some affection of the brain. It came upon us so unexpectedly and suddenly. Nell is broken hearted. I fear much for her health. You know how her heart was wrapped up in her dear boy."

One year later—July 25, 1864—Ellen Arthur gave birth to another child, Chester Alan Arthur II. The Arthurs called him Alan and doted on the boy, fearful that he might die as well.

CHAPTER FOUR

POSTWAR POLITICS

I am confident that my appointment [to a government job] can be made very satisfactory to our friends here, & I need not say that you have no more faithful or attached friend than myself.
—Chester Arthur to Edwin Morgan, January 24, 1866

The Civil War continued to take a terrible toll. Between the death of Arthur's first son and the birth of his second, tens of thousands of soldiers and civilians died. By 1864 Northerners and Southerners alike were weary of war.

In September 1864, Chester Arthur found out that his brother, William, who was a doctor in the Union army, had been shot during a battle in Virginia. Arthur went to Washington, D.C., and found his brother in a hospital there. William had been shot in the face and was nearly deaf. As soon as William could travel, Arthur brought him back to New York City. With the help of Edwin Morgan, by then a U.S. senator, Arthur found a permanent position for his brother in the U.S. Army. William became a paymaster, responsible for military finances.

Since becoming adults, both brothers had rarely visited their parents. They left their sisters to take care of the aging couple, although Chester sometimes stopped by when he was on business in Albany. Neither brother was as religious as Elder Arthur would have liked. Malvina Arthur, their mother, wrote long letters to them, urging them to become better Christians.

In the fall of 1864, Arthur helped collect money for Abraham Lincoln's presidential reelection. Some Northerners were losing confidence in the president. Many doubted that Lincoln would win a second term. But in November 1864, Union general William Tecumseh Sherman captured Atlanta, Georgia—an important victory for the North. The victory boosted support for Lincoln, and he won reelection.

The Republicans returned to power in New York State. Roscoe Conkling regained his seat in the House of

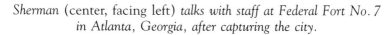

Sherman (center, facing left) *talks with staff at Federal Fort No. 7 in Atlanta, Georgia, after capturing the city.*

Representatives, and Republican Reuben Fenton was elected governor. Arthur tried to get back his former position as inspector general in the New York State militia. But Fenton gave the job to someone else. So Arthur continued to practice law.

By January 1865, transportation problems had crippled the South. Union troops blocked shipments of food and equipment bound for Confederate territory. The Confederate forces—and many civilians—were barely surviving. General Sherman marched his troops through North Carolina and South Carolina, destroying homes and crops in his path.

Finally, on April 9, 1865, Confederate general Robert E. Lee surrendered to Union general Ulysses S. Grant. Although

Sherman's troops burned much of Charleston, South Carolina, including the railroad depot (above), in order to crush the spirit of the South.

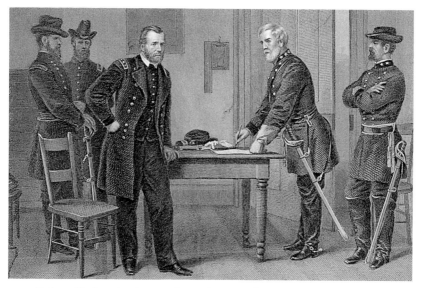

Robert E. Lee (right, with pen) *surrenders to Ulysses S. Grant* (hatless, at left) *at Appomattox Court House in Virginia.*

fighting continued for several more weeks, the Civil War was officially over. Five days later, a southern actor named John Wilkes Booth shot and killed President Lincoln. Andrew Johnson, the vice president, became president.

CLIMBING THE PATRONAGE LADDER

Chester Arthur continued to strengthen his political connections. He handled lawsuits involving the recently ended war and worked hard to prosper. In May he bought a large house at 123 Lexington Avenue, in a fashionable area of New York City. He hired Irish immigrants as servants to help with household chores and with caring for young Alan.

By 1865 the executive branch of the federal government employed about fifty-three thousand people, half of whom worked for the postal service. The Treasury Department also had many employees. Most jobs were awarded as part of the patronage system. That is, officeholders gave jobs to their political supporters and allies.

Arthur was eager to move up to a federal patronage job. He helped a wealthy business associate named Tom Murphy get elected to the New York state legislature in the fall of 1865. For his assistance, he hoped to be rewarded with an appointment to a well-paying federal job. But by then, William Marcy Tweed (known as Boss Tweed) had replaced Thurlow Weed as the power broker in Republican politics. Despite help from Murphy, Morgan, and others, Arthur didn't get an appointment.

Arthur kept trying. His law partner, Henry Gardiner, had recently died, and Arthur had few clients. He spent a lot of

✧ ————————————

Boss Tweed controlled New York City politics throughout the 1860s.

time at Tom Murphy's Thirty-ninth Street home, which had become the informal headquarters of Conkling's faction of the Republican Party. There, Arthur enjoyed cigars, whiskey, and the company of fellow Republicans. In 1867 he was elected to join the Century Club, an exclusive group of New York's most influential men. Arthur drank and dined with famous actors, university presidents, and bankers.

STALWARTS, RADICALS, AND HALF-BREEDS

Roscoe Conkling became a U.S. senator on March 4, 1867. Chester Arthur continued his involvement with New York City politics. The city was divided into hundreds of voting districts and twenty-one assembly districts (which included twenty-five to thirty-five voting districts each). Arthur became the Republican representative in the Eighteenth Assembly District. He also joined the Republican Party's citywide Central Committee. In this position, he helped set party policy and support party members in elections. In 1868 Arthur became chairman of the committee.

Because Conkling supported Ulysses S. Grant for the presidency, Arthur did too. They collected campaign contributions and worked to ensure that Grant received New York's votes at the Republican National Convention in Chicago in May 1868. They also worked to finance Grant's victory in the general election that November.

Conkling's faction of the Republican Party became known as the Stalwarts because they claimed to be stalwart (loyal and dependable) supporters of President Grant. Other Republicans—led by James Blaine—were sometimes called Radicals because they favored taking harsh measures against the defeated southern states.

But Conkling's Stalwarts had another name for Blaine's Radical Republicans: Half-Breeds. Stalwarts argued that the Radical Republicans half supported President Grant but half supported reforming Grant's system of patronage and machine politics. In fact, the Stalwarts and the Half-Breeds were not very different when it came to their policies for the Republican Party.

THE FIGHT FOR WOMAN'S RIGHTS

Originally, the U.S. Constitution gave voting rights only to adult white men. Many U.S. and state laws denied women other basic rights, such as the right to own property. In the nineteenth century, women began to demand change. They wanted the right to vote and other rights that men enjoyed.

In 1869 Elizabeth Cady Stanton and Susan B. Anthony formed the National Woman Suffrage (voting rights) Association. The same year, Lucy Stone and her followers formed the American Woman Suffrage Association.

The Fifteenth Amendment to the U.S. Constitution went into effect in 1870. This amendment gave voting rights to African American men, but not to women of any race. Women were angry. They continued to fight for the right to vote and other rights.

The National Woman Suffrage Association and the American Woman Suffrage Association eventually merged. They formed the National American Woman Suffrage Association. The group continued to work for universal U.S. woman suffrage. (The Nineteenth Amendment achieved this goal in 1920.)

What separated them most was the personal hatred between their two leaders.

At this same time, southern states—once again part of the Union—were trying to recover from the ravages of the Civil War. The postwar period was known as Reconstruction, because the U.S. government created programs to reconstruct the South. During this period, Congress oversaw the creation of new governments in southern states. It also passed laws to protect the rights of former slaves. The Fourteenth Amendment to the U.S. Constitution went into effect in 1868. This amendment said that everyone born in the United States, including former slaves, were citizens. It prohibited states from denying any citizen equal protection of the law.

On January 16, 1869, Chester Arthur went to Newtonville, New York, to be with his sick mother, Malvina. She died that evening. According to one of his sisters, "when he saw Mother he sat down and wept like a child."

CHAPTER FIVE

SUCCESS IN THE GILDED AGE

No country can be well governed unless its citizens . . . keep religiously before their minds that they are the guardians of the law, and that the law officers are only the machinery for its execution, nothing more.
—Mark Twain and Charles Dudley Warner, *The Gilded Age, 1873*

Chester Arthur's work for the Stalwarts finally paid off. In 1869 Tom Murphy arranged for Boss Tweed to create a new state government position—the office of counsel (legal adviser) to the New York City Tax Commission. Tweed appointed Arthur to the job. He earned a huge salary of $10,000 (about $125,000) per year. Skilled workers of that era got salaries that ranged from about $400 ($5,000) to $650 ($8,125) per year. In addition to this, he still made money from his law practice. Despite the high pay, Arthur hoped that President Grant would give him an even better patronage job as a reward for his loyalty and effort.

President Grant knew that the nation's civil service (government employment) system needed reform. In March 1870, he established the Civil Service Commission to explore ways to get rid of the spoils system. The commission investigated one place that had a reputation for corruption—the customhouse for the Port of New York.

In 1871 most of the goods other nations shipped to the United States landed in New York City. The United States collected customs (import taxes and other fees) on these goods. These fees served two purposes. They brought money into the U.S. Treasury, and they made foreign products more expensive than U.S.-made goods, thereby encouraging people to buy from U.S. businesses. The United States had several customhouses and ports of entry, but the New York Customhouse was the largest and most important. It collected about three-quarters of all the customs money for the nation.

But the system was corrupt. Customs officials often took bribes. They were required to give assessments—part of their salaries, also called kickbacks—to the politicians who had given them jobs. They were also supposed to donate their time and energy to help their political party.

Legally, customs officials had the right to seize illegal goods smuggled into the United States, to fine importers who broke the law, and to sell goods left in the customhouse that no one had claimed. In what was called the moiety system, customs officials sometimes kept a portion of fines or money from the sale of illegal and unclaimed goods.

Chester Arthur's associate Tom Murphy was in charge of the New York Customhouse. Murphy had a reputation for

THE GILDED AGE

The Gilded Age was an era in U.S. history that lasted from the end of the Civil War to the start of the 1900s. The name comes from an 1873 novel—*The Gilded Age*—written by Mark Twain and Charles Dudley Warner. The story describes the business successes and failures of three young people out to make their fortunes. It includes corrupt politicians, very much like those Chester Arthur knew.

Gilded means covered in gold. During this era, many Americans grew fantastically rich. Corporations, manufacturing firms, and railroads were on the rise. Big business allied with politicians to rig elections and to win favors from one another. Rich Americans such as Chester Arthur flaunted their wealth, wore expensive clothes, and decorated their homes lavishly. But while the rich grew richer, the poor remained poor. Immigrants crowded into city slums. Many working people struggled just to survive.

being one of the most corrupt spoilsmen. Pressed to do so by President Grant and his advisers, Murphy resigned his position in November 1871. New York's Senator Conkling and his Stalwart followers encouraged Grant to appoint Chester Arthur to take Murphy's place.

Arthur's possible appointment met with mixed reviews. Some newspaper editorials recalled his years of good service to New York as an attorney and as quartermaster during the Civil War. Others worried that Arthur was too close to Murphy and Conkling to act independently of these men. Horace Greeley, an editor and prominent Democrat, wrote:

"Personally, he is a gentleman and a man of education, but the fact that he is a prominent member of the Customhouse faction forbids the hope that he will take the Customhouse out of politics or institute any real reform." Despite such criticisms, President Grant went ahead with the appointment.

GENTLEMAN BOSS

On November 21, 1871, Ellen Arthur gave birth to a daughter, named Ellen Herndon Arthur in her mother's honor. Little Nell joined her brother Alan, aged seven. That same day, newspapers announced that Chester Arthur would take over Tom Murphy's job at the New York Customhouse. On December 1, Arthur assumed his duties at a huge granite building on Wall Street in lower Manhattan.

——————— ✧
Arthur handled import taxes and fees in his duties at the New York Customhouse (right).

Arthur headed up the Collections Department, which handled import taxes and fees. He worked with three other heads of departments at the customhouse—the surveyor, the naval officer, and the appraiser. All four officials were appointed for four-year terms. Arthur's job as collector was by far the most important.

In a short time, Arthur got a reputation for being friendly, tactful, and open with everyone he met. He could talk with the most powerful businessman importing goods into the United States to the least important of the thousand or so clerks who helped run the Collections Department. But soon Greeley's prediction came true. Arthur gave customhouse jobs to many Stalwart Republicans. And although his salary was considerably less, his income soared to about $55,000 ($775,000) a year. Most of this money came from the moiety system. (There is no evidence that Arthur took bribes or kickbacks.) By comparison, the president's salary was also $55,000 dollars. The vice president's was only $10,000 ($140,000).

Soon after Arthur took charge of the New York Customhouse, the Civil Service Commission began setting rules for government employees. In October 1872, the commission tried to ban the practice of assessments. Arthur admitted, in a letter to the commission, that customhouse employees did pay assessments, but he claimed that he had only recently learned about them.

Silas Burt thought otherwise. He had gone to Union College about the same time as Arthur had, and the two men had recently renewed their friendship. When Burt confronted Arthur about corrupt activities, Arthur replied: "You are one of those goody-goody fellows who set up a high standard of morality [right and wrong] that other people cannot reach."

The reputation Ulysses S. Grant (right) had as a Civil War general helped him win two presidential elections.

──────────── ✧

CHET THE COLLECTOR

In 1872 Ulysses Grant ran for reelection against Democrat Horace Greeley. Grant won a landslide victory. A Republican became governor of New York, and in January 1873, the New York state legislature voted to return Roscoe Conkling to the U.S. Senate. (At the time, state legislatures, not state voters, elected senators.) The Republicans held the White House and had a slim advantage in Congress—and the Stalwarts dominated the Republican Party.

By then Reconstruction efforts in the South were winding down. At the same time, some white southerners used terror and violence to keep African Americans from voting and running for political office. U.S. troops tried to keep the peace and protect African Americans. But many southerners deeply resented the interference of these soldiers.

In 1873 the country entered a depression, or economic downturn. Times were hard for many. When congressmen voted to increase their own salaries for the second time in one year, the public was outraged. Congress reversed its decision.

Sensing the mood of the country, Congress passed the Anti-Moiety Act of 1874. This act prohibited customs officials from sharing in fines, penalties, or sales money. Under the new law, Arthur's income as collector would be limited to $12,000 ($180,000)—his official salary.

However, the Arthurs continued to maintain an upper-middle-class lifestyle. Their large home on Lexington Avenue had expensive furnishings. They employed five servants to run the household. The family took costly vacations, and the children had private tutors.

Arthur enjoyed going on fishing expeditions with his friends. He often stayed up until the early morning hours, drinking and smoking cigars with business and political associates at Delmonico's restaurant or the Fifth Avenue

———————— ✧
Delmonico's restaurant (right) was a popular spot for the powerful in New York.

Hotel. Silas Burt wrote that Arthur "was absent from home on evenings almost continually, [and rose from bed] late in the mornings." The collector often got to the customhouse three hours after it opened for business.

By this time, Arthur's late-night drinking and eating had caused him to balloon above 225 pounds. He still carried himself in an elegant manner. He dressed in the latest British fashions and had suits and hats specially imported from London, England. He required his son Alan to call him Sir.

Ellen Arthur, about a hundred pounds lighter than her husband, entertained lavishly at home and sang at charity functions. She kept a record of who came to dinner, maintaining the social connections her husband needed to rise in his career. Although Arthur rarely spent time with his family, except on vacations, Ellen did not criticize him in public. She went to the opera with friends, enjoyed horseback riding, and put on a bright, merry face. Only in private did she admit to feeling sad and angry about her husband's behavior.

Arthur's father had remarried after Arthur's mother died. Arthur saw his father for the last time in Newtonville in the fall of 1875. Shortly afterward, Elder Arthur died. Arthur also kept in touch with his brother, William.

A TARNISHED REPUTATION

Arthur finished his four-year term as collector on December 10, 1875. He had been popular with nearly everyone with whom he did business. By then Roscoe Conkling chaired the Senate Commerce Committee, which approved the president's nominations for government jobs in the nation's ports and harbors. With Conkling's support, Arthur easily won a second term as collector.

Roscoe Conkling wanted to run for president, and Arthur supported him at the Republican National Convention in June 1876. James Blaine and others were interested in the nomination as well. After several rounds of ballot-ing, convention delegates finally chose Ohio gover-nor Rutherford B. Hayes as the nominee. His vice-presidential running mate was William Wheeler, a congressman from New York. Hayes's Democratic opponent was New York governor Samuel Tilden.

Rutherford B. Hayes

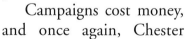

Campaigns cost money, and once again, Chester Arthur had to support his party. Despite efforts at civil ser-vice reform, the assessment system still flourished at the New York Customhouse and elsewhere. Joseph Pinckney, one of Arthur's Republican associates, kept a list of every-one with a job in the New York Customhouse. These people were expected to "donate" 4 or 5 percent of their salaries to the presidential campaign. Pinckney received the money in an office on Hanover Street, nicknamed Hand-Over Street.

The election of 1876 was so close that a special congres-sional committee decided the outcome. In what became

An Electoral Commission was set up to decide whether Hayes or Tilden would become president. It announced its decision in March 1877.

known as the Compromise of 1876, the Democrats agreed that Hayes, not Tilden, would become president. In exchange, the Republicans agreed to withdraw remaining federal troops from the South. Reconstruction was over.

Both Democrats and Republicans had campaigned in favor of a more honest method of filling government jobs. President Hayes ordered an investigation of the New York Customhouse. As part of the investigation, Arthur went to Washington, D.C., in April 1877. He met with Treasury secretary John Sherman and testified before an investigating group called the Jay Commission. Arthur told the commission that he felt pressure to give jobs to friends and relatives of important businessmen and politicians. He admitted that there were problems in the New York Customhouse but noted that the organization was no worse than other customhouses throughout the nation.

In a series of reports from May through August 1877, the Jay Commission found that the New York Customhouse was overstaffed and that some senior officers were corrupt. Secretary Sherman ordered Arthur to reduce his staff. President Hayes also banned federal employees—including customhouse officials—from paying assessments to political parties and from working on political campaigns.

To completely clean up the customhouse, Hayes's staff wanted Arthur to resign as collector. Secretary Sherman even offered Arthur a government job in Paris if he resigned. Arthur turned him down. He fought to keep his job, but there was too much opposition. On February 3, 1878, the Senate voted to replace Arthur with Edwin Merritt.

Chester Arthur returned to his law practice. In April 1878, Ellen Arthur, six-year-old Little Nell, and a maid sailed for France. Nell had hoped to see her mother, Frances Hansbrough Herndon, who was living there at the time. But they arrived too late. Frances died before they got there. Despite their grief, the family shopped for the latest French fashions. They also visited several of Nell's relatives and returned with Frances Herndon's remains for burial in Virginia. Nell also returned with a small inheritance.

SUDDEN LOSS

Despite his ouster from the customhouse, Chester Arthur continued to increase his political influence. In February 1879, he became president of New York State's Republican Central Committee. Arthur's friend Tom Murphy became the committee's treasurer.

Roscoe Conkling started his second term in the U.S. Senate in March 1879. That year, for the first time, all the major state elections—for governor, legislators, and other state officials—were held at the same time in New York. Arthur was in charge of collecting campaign contributions.

Despite the push for reform, Arthur and other party officials raised money in the traditional way. The Central Committee pressured party members for contributions. Arthur also found speakers to pound home the "vote Republican" message throughout New York State. And his work paid off. Republican candidates won every election in New York except for state engineer.

Arthur was meeting with state legislators in Albany on Sunday, January 11, 1880, when he got a telegram urging him to return to New York City. His wife had caught

✧ ————————————
Ellen Herndon Arthur
enjoyed dressing fashionably
up until her death.

pneumonia while waiting outside for a carriage after a concert. She was gravely ill.

Arthur caught the only train home from Albany that day, but it didn't arrive until evening. By then the doctor had given Ellen a painkiller called morphine. She was unconscious. Arthur stayed by her bedside until she died on January 12. She was just forty-two years old. Arthur was overcome with grief.

The funeral, at Fifth Avenue's Church of the Heavenly Rest, was filled with well-wishers. A train carried Ellen's coffin to Albany, where New York's governor and legislators attended the burial in the Arthur family plot in the parklike Albany Rural Cemetery.

CHAPTER SIX

"A GREATER HONOR"

*I have known [Chester Arthur] for twenty-five
years . . . and a more loyal party man and true
Republican cannot be found anywhere.*
—Thurlow Weed, June 1880

Politics had kept Arthur from his wife and family, and it was
to politics that he returned after Ellen's death. Since 1880 was
a presidential election year, Arthur was a busy man. President
Hayes had announced that he would not run for reelection.

The Republican National Convention was scheduled to
begin on June 2 in Chicago. Arthur arrived five days early
to prepare. The Stalwarts were backing the nomination of
former president Grant, who wanted to run for a third
term. The Half-Breeds—who by then used this name
proudly—wanted the nomination to go to Maine senator
James Blaine (Roscoe Conkling's bitter rival).

On Monday, June 7, the convention's nearly fifteen
thousand delegates jammed into a building called the Glass

*Thousands attended the 1880 Republican National
Convention at Chicago's Glass Palace.*

Palace. The first round of balloting that morning revealed a
deeply divided party. With 379 votes needed to win the
nomination, Blaine got 284 and Grant got 304. On the
second ballot, the Pennsylvania delegation gave one vote to
James Garfield, an Ohio congressman who had not openly
sided with either Stalwarts or Half-Breeds.

Ballot after ballot, no candidate could get enough
votes to win. About noon on Tuesday, thirty-three ballots
later, Garfield looked like the compromise candidate.
Blaine and the Half-Breeds threw their support behind
him. Once Conkling was assured that the nomination for
vice president would go to a Stalwart from New York, he

James A. Garfield was the compromise candidate at the 1880 Republican National Convention.

——————— ✧

supported Garfield as well. On ballot thirty-six, the deal was done. James Garfield became the Republicans' candidate for president. No one knew who the vice-presidential candidate would be, except that it would be a Stalwart New Yorker who could deliver New York voters to the Republicans.

Garfield asked New York banker Levi Morton to be his running mate. Morton asked Conkling whether he should accept the offer. Conkling vetoed the idea, most likely because he thought Garfield would lose in the general election and that would make Morton look like a loser too.

Then someone in the Ohio delegation asked Chester Arthur if he was interested in the vice presidency. Honored to be asked, Arthur said yes. A member of the New York delegation overheard the conversation and later told fellow delegate Tom Murphy.

Murphy grabbed a carriage and raced to the Grand Pacific Hotel, where Conkling and Arthur were staying. The three men met in private. Conkling, thinking that Garfield would lose the national election, told Arthur not to accept Garfield's proposal. But Arthur replied, "The office of the Vice-President is a greater honor than I ever dreamed of attaining."

Despite Conkling's discouragement, Arthur vowed to accept the nomination and to make sure that most of New York's delegates voted for him. Conkling turned his back on his friend and left. Arthur stayed at the hotel, and Murphy rushed back to the convention.

Under pressure from Murphy, the New York delegation met at 3:30 on June 8. The group approved Arthur's nomination by voice vote. Angry with Arthur, Conkling stayed away from the convention and didn't cast a vote.

Garfield and Arthur then met at the Grand Pacific Hotel. The two men, both trained as lawyers, stood together and shook hands with party members for two hours. Afterward,

Crossed Paths to the White House

Garfield and Arthur barely knew each other when they became running mates on the Republican ticket. But their paths had almost crossed once before. In 1854 Garfield had taught penmanship to students in the North Pownal school where Arthur had been the principal until 1852. Like Arthur, Garfield taught school to earn money to study law.

Arthur's hand swelled so much that a ring had to be cut off one of his fingers.

A CLOSE RACE

Arthur's nomination gave Republicans a good chance of winning a majority of votes in New York. Some worried that Arthur, because he was linked to corrupt practices in New York City and the New York Customhouse, might hurt Garfield's chance of winning the presidency. But one politician reasoned that the ticket would benefit from Arthur as "the shrewdest political manager in the country."

Arthur returned home by train on June 11. Crowds cheered and congratulated him as he made his way to the house on Lexington Avenue. His daughter, eight-year-old Nell, gave him a bouquet of flowers. But Arthur was saddened that his wife was not there to

Nell Arthur

✧

share in his good fortune. According his sister Regina, "When [the flowers] were brought on to the [dinner] table and Chester called little Nell to him to kiss her, he completely broke down and said 'there is nothing worth having now.'" By the time guests came to the house shortly after

dinner, however, Arthur greeted them in his usual charming, sophisticated manner.

The next night, about twenty-five hundred people stood
in front of the Fifth Avenue Hotel, where Arthur was meeting with other politicians. The crowd chanted, "Arthur!
Arthur!" When he appeared on the balcony, a band played
"Hail to the Chief."

The Democrats nominated war hero Winfield Hancock of
Pennsylvania as their presidential candidate. William English,
a former congressman from Indiana, was the Democratic candidate for the vice presidency. The Greenback Party, which
backed the issuance of paper money, nominated Civil War
general James Weaver for president. The Prohibition Party,
which wanted to ban the sale of alcoholic beverages, nominated businessman Neal Dow. Weaver and Dow were not

◇ ————————
*Winfield Hancock was the
Democratic presidential
nominee in 1880.*

expected to win, however. Most observers focused on the race between Garfield and Hancock.

Garfield and Arthur had never been political allies. Arthur was a Stalwart, and Garfield, as it turned out, favored the Half-Breeds. The two men actually disliked and distrusted each other. They spent little time together before Election Day.

While Garfield spent most of the campaign receiving visitors at his home in Mentor, Ohio, Arthur took to the campaign trail. He coordinated rallies for the Republican Party.

An 1880 campaign poster shows Garfield and Arthur amid patriotic images.

He arranged for Grant and Conkling to drum up votes in Ohio and Indiana—two states that were crucial for the Republicans to win. He sent a close political ally, Stephen Dorsey, to Indiana to get Republican votes any way he could. Arthur also assessed Republican government workers 3 percent of their annual salaries as campaign contributions.

About three-quarters of the nation's eligible voters—the largest percentage ever recorded in a U.S. presidential election—cast their ballots on November 2, 1880. The Garfield-Arthur ticket barely won the popular vote (4,454,416 to 4,444,852), including the majority of votes in New York and Indiana. If Arthur and Dorsey hadn't "delivered" these states to Garfield, the election would have gone to Hancock. Some people thought the Republicans had broken the law to win the election, but Hancock did not challenge the result. (Weaver got about 300,000 votes, and Dow about 10,000.)

ARTHUR TAKES OFFICE

Arthur joined Garfield for the inaugural celebration on a cold, snowy March 4, 1881. Crowds cheered as the presidential and vice-presidential carriages made their way from the White House to the Capitol. Arthur made a short speech and was sworn in as vice president. Garfield gave a longer address, then took the oath as president. A reporter noted that "Gen. Arthur, strong, keen-eyed, and handsome as ever, and because of his commanding form and military bearing [was] a central attraction." Widowed for more than a year, Arthur attended the lavish inaugural ball that evening. He arrived at about 9:00 P.M. and shook hands until nearly midnight.

Garfield takes the oath of office in front of the Capitol on March 4, 1881. Arthur is seated on the far right.

———————— ✧

As vice president, Arthur presided over the Senate. That meant he could cast a vote to break a tie among the senators. The Senate was evenly divided that year between Democrats and Republicans, so it was likely that Arthur's tiebreaking Republican vote would become important.

Even more important was President Garfield's cabinet, or team of advisers. Each cabinet member headed a U.S. government department, such as the Department of the Treasury and Department of State. The Half-Breeds and the Stalwarts each wanted to control these positions.

Chester Arthur and Roscoe Conkling shared an apartment in Washington, D.C. Both were upset when, right after the inauguration, the president announced that James Blaine, the leader of the Half-Breeds, would be his secretary of state. Levi Morton, a Stalwart who had raised large sums for the campaign, expected Garfield to make him secretary of the treasury. But Garfield gave the job to U.S. senator William Windom of Minnesota.

During the first week of the Garfield-Arthur administration, hundreds of men came to the White House, hoping for a position with the U.S. government. Garfield met with many of them personally. Among them was a quiet young man who sided with the Stalwart faction of Republicans. His name was Charles Guiteau.

Guiteau gave the president a copy of a pro-Garfield speech he claimed to have delivered during the campaign. On the front cover, he had written the words "Paris consulship." This was a diplomatic position, representing the United States in France, that Guiteau hoped to obtain. As Garfield started to read the speech, Guiteau quietly left. He felt certain that he would be one Stalwart who would get a good job in the new administration.

CHAPTER SEVEN

FRIGHTFUL RESPONSIBILITY

*The most frightful responsibility which
ever [fell] upon any one would be the
casting of the Presidency upon me.*
—Chester Arthur, September 1881

While Charles Guiteau waited with growing impatience for
his appointment to Paris, the battle between Stalwarts and
Half-Breeds centered on a plum job that had once been
Chester Arthur's—collector for the New York Customhouse.
Secretary of State James Blaine advised Garfield to appoint
William Robertson to the job. Robertson was a Half-Breed,
and he was expected to fill the customhouse with his supporters. The result would be fewer jobs for Stalwarts and
less power for Roscoe Conkling. Conkling and his fellow
senator from New York, Tom Platt, were dead set against
Robertson getting the job. So was Arthur.

Because this was an important U.S. government job,
Robertson's appointment had to be approved by the Senate.

Republican senators were caught in the middle—wanting to support the new president but unwilling to defy their colleagues from New York. Weeks went by with the Senate stalled over Robertson's nomination.

The feud between Conkling supporters and Garfield supporters made headlines day after day, as Stalwarts and Half-Breeds tried to maneuver for power. Meanwhile, Charles Guiteau—getting more desperate for a job and more certain that he deserved one—grew increasingly angry with the Half-Breeds.

"HE IS SOBBING LIKE A CHILD"

On July 2, 1881, President Garfield got ready to leave the White House for summer vacation. He and Secretary of State Blaine went to the Baltimore and Potomac railroad depot. As the president walked through the waiting room toward his train, Charles Guiteau took aim with an

In this illustration, Charles Guiteau (left) shoots President Garfield (center) at the Washington, D.C., railroad depot on July 2, 1881.

English bulldog pistol. He then shot Garfield in the arm and back. Afterward, Guiteau was heard to shout: "I am a Stalwart and Arthur will be President!" A doctor soon rushed to the scene. Garfield, gravely wounded, was carried to the White House.

Arthur learned about the assassination attempt just as he and Conkling returned to New York City from Albany by Hudson River steamboat. They went to Conkling's room in the Fifth Avenue Hotel, then Arthur returned to his Lexington Avenue house. Throughout the day, Blaine sent him telegrams, describing the president's critical condition. "What can I say?" Arthur remarked to a reporter. "I am overwhelmed by grief over the awful news."

At the urging of Blaine and the rest of the president's cabinet, Arthur took the midnight train to Washington, arriving at eight o'clock the next morning. He met briefly with cabinet members, telling them, "God knows I do not want the place [the presidency] I was never elected to."

Guiteau had been captured minutes after shooting Garfield and was being held in a local jail. Investigators found a letter Guiteau had addressed to "President Arthur," confessing to the assassination and recommending changes in the cabinet. The day after the shooting, the *New York Times* reported that Guiteau had told a detective: "Arthur and all those men are my friends." Rumors spread that the Stalwarts had hired Guiteau. Though the rumors were untrue and few people believed them, some blamed the Stalwarts for the patronage system in which Guiteau thought he deserved a government job.

Arthur was deeply hurt by the attacks on him and distressed at the thought of taking over the presidency in this

manner. He stayed at the Washington home of Nevada senator John P. Jones for more than a week. Only after doctors
announced that President Garfield's condition had improved
did Arthur return to New York City. He remained there for
the rest of the summer, awaiting daily bulletins of President
Garfield's condition.

With Congress on summer break, the nation's government
came to a near standstill. There was one important develop-
ment. William Robertson was confirmed as customhouse collector. On August 1, he officially started in Arthur's former
job in the New York Customhouse.

On September 6, to get relief from the Washington,
D.C., heat, Garfield traveled by train to a cottage on the
seashore in Elberon, New Jersey. Thousands of people stood
by the railroad tracks to watch the train go by. Garfield

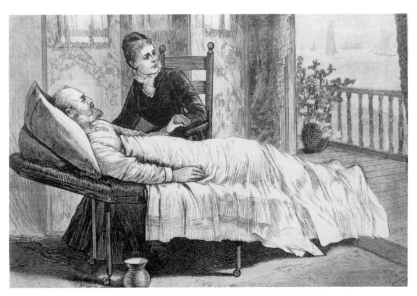

Garfield's health improved briefly at the seashore in New Jersey.

seemed to improve for a few days. Then, suffering from a massive infection and in constant pain, the president died at 10:35 P.M. on September 19, 1881.

A messenger soon brought the news to Arthur. Then came a telegram from the cabinet: "It becomes our painful duty to advise you to take the oath of office as President of the United States without delay. We will be very glad if you will come here on the earliest train tomorrow morning."

Reporters gathered at the front entrance to Arthur's home. Arthur's doorkeeper, Alec Powell, told them: "He is sitting alone in his room sobbing like a child, with his head on his desk and his face buried in his hands. I dare not disturb him." Arthur's son, Alan, arrived home about midnight. Several friends went to find a judge who could officially swear in Arthur as president. At 2:15 in the morning,

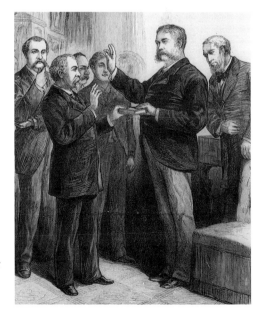

——————— ✧

Judge John R. Brady administers the oath of office to Arthur in Arthur's New York City home.

Judge John R. Brady of the New York Supreme Court administered the oath of office to the new president.

MR. PRESIDENT

Arthur went to Elberon to meet with Mrs. Garfield and cabinet members and to accompany Garfield's body back to Washington. On September 22, he took another oath of office, this one administered in the Capitol by Morrison Waite, chief justice of the Supreme Court. Arthur gave a short speech, noting: "Men may die, but the fabrics of our free institutions remain unshaken. . . . Summoned to these high duties and responsibilities and profoundly conscious of the magnitude and gravity, I assume the trust imposed by the Constitution, relying for aid on divine guidance and the virtue, patriotism, and intelligence of the American people." His first official act as the twenty-first president of the United States was to declare the day of Garfield's funeral, September 26, 1881, a national day of mourning.

Julia Sand, who had sent an encouraging letter to Arthur in August, wrote him again when he became president. She urged Arthur to proceed slowly. "What the nation needs most at present," she wrote, "is rest."

But rest was not possible. Everyone in Garfield's cabinet, except Secretary of War Robert Todd Lincoln (Abraham Lincoln's son), resigned shortly after Arthur took office. They thought the new president should pick his own cabinet. Arthur had to find a new team.

For years and years, Arthur had followed the lead of Roscoe Conkling. Naturally, many thought that Arthur would give Conkling a cabinet post, probably replacing Blaine as secretary of state. In that position, Conkling would

Arthur chose Frederick Frelinghuysen (left) to be his secretary of state.

✧ ———————

help Arthur with trade and relations with other nations. Instead, Arthur chose Frederick Frelinghuysen, a well-respected attorney from New Jersey, as the new secretary of state. Unlike Blaine or Conkling, Frelinghuysen was quiet, conservative, and skilled at working tactfully toward peace.

Many people were surprised to learn that Arthur did not offer any cabinet position to Conkling. And if that were not surprising enough, Arthur also kept William Robertson as collector in the New York Customhouse. President Arthur was determined to show that he could act independently and rise above spoilsmen politics.

GETTING DOWN TO BUSINESS
But Arthur didn't lose his taste for fine living. The White House was in sore need of renovations, and Arthur asked Louis C. Tiffany, a well-known decorator from New York,

Louis C. Tiffany (right) *was in charge of the White House renovations in 1881.*
—————— ✧

to take charge. As soon as the Garfield family left, twenty-four wagonloads of furniture and household objects from former presidents—including a pair of Abraham Lincoln's pants—were cleared away and sold at public auction. During the renovations, Arthur lived in Senator Jones's mansion. He set up his office on the second floor. His private secretary, Fred Phillips, and most of the White House clerical staff had offices on the first floor.

On December 6, President Arthur delivered his first annual message to Congress, which had just started a new session. Arthur proposed that lawmakers take on important tasks, such as improving the National Board of Health, protecting the property rights of Native Americans, and strengthening the U.S. Navy.

ARTHUR AND NATIVE AMERICANS

Throughout much of its history, the United States expanded westward. To clear land for white farmers, miners, and ranchers, U.S. soldiers did battle with Native Americans, whose families had lived on western lands for generations. Soldiers killed thousands of Native Americans. Those who were not killed were rounded up and forced to live on lands called reservations. Many Native Americans died of starvation and disease during this period.

By some estimates, as many as ten million Native Americans once lived on lands that would become the modern United States. By the time Chester Arthur became president, only a few hundred thousand Native Americans remained in the nation.

Chester Arthur opposed the poor treatment of Native Americans. "The Indian [Native American] should receive the protection of the law," Arthur argued. "He should be allowed to maintain in court his rights of person and property."

At the same time, Arthur did not respect the unique, centuries-old culture of Native Americans. Instead, he wanted to "absorb [Native Americans] into the mass of our [white] citizens." He and Henry Teller, secretary of the interior, supported the creation of Indian schools that would teach Native American children about white society. At these schools, Native American students learned English, dressed in the style of white Americans, and learned about Christianity and Anglo-American traditions. They were forbidden to use their native languages or to practice their native customs. By 1884 about 160 Indian schools were operating in the United States.

He also gave a detailed accounting of government activities from July 1, 1880, to June 30, 1881. The accounting included every penny of U.S. Treasury income: $360,782,292.57. Government spending had been much lower, leaving a surplus of $100,069,404.98. What to do with that surplus was an important topic for the nation.

The next day, Arthur and his family moved into the White House. By then, Alan was a seventeen-year-old freshman at the College of New Jersey (later renamed Princeton University). Nell was ten. Because Arthur was a widow, his youngest sister, Mary Arthur McElroy, agreed to be the official White House hostess. In this job, she arranged social events and welcomed guests. Mary's daughter May was Nell's age, and the two cousins sometimes livened up White House parties and receptions.

✧ ————————————
Charles Guiteau (left)
was accused and convicted
of the assassination of
James Garfield.

GUITEAU ON TRIAL

As Arthur worked to master his duties as president, public attention turned to the murder trial of Charles Guiteau. The trial, which began in November 1881, dragged on into January of 1882.

Guiteau had met Arthur at least once during the 1880 campaign. He testified that he "used to go to General Arthur and talk just as freely with him as I would with anybody." Guiteau also wrote to Arthur, asking him to tell the prosecution (government lawyers) to go easy on him. He admitted to shooting Garfield, but he argued that the bullet wound had not been the cause of death. Instead, he claimed, the president had died from poor medical treatment and because it was God's will that he should die. On January 25, Guiteau was convicted of killing Garfield and later sentenced to hang.

President Arthur worked hard to separate himself from spoilsmen politics and do what he believed was right for the country.

CHAPTER EIGHT

HIS OWN MAN

*Deeply impressed with the gravity of the
responsibilities which have so unexpectedly
[fallen] upon me, it will be my constant
purpose to cooperate with [Congress] in such
measures as will promote the glory of the
country and the prosperity of its people.*
—Chester Arthur, December 1881

President Arthur took his job seriously. He studied reports
from his cabinet members and asked Congress to pass laws
that would benefit the nation. But Congress did not act on
most of Arthur's proposals. Arthur was in a weak position
politically. He had not been elected president, and about as
many Democrats as Republicans were in Congress. But
Arthur did have one powerful tool—the presidential veto. If
Congress passed a bill (proposed law), he could refuse to
sign it into law. Congress could then enact the bill into law
only if at least two-thirds of the House and the Senate

voted to override the veto. These votes were hard to get with Congress so evenly divided.

President Arthur used his veto power on April 4, 1882. He refused to sign a bill that limited the number of Chinese immigrants who could come to the United States. The bill further banned Chinese laborers from entering the United States for twenty years. The bill also denied U.S. citizenship to Chinese residents. Because of its racist provisions, Arthur thought the bill was "undemocratic and hostile to the spirit of our institutions." He also considered the bill an insult to China, which had just signed a trade agreement with the United States. Congress drafted another bill that shortened the ban on Chinese laborers to ten years. The bill was popular with the public, and Arthur felt pressured to sign it. So on May 6, the president reluctantly signed the Chinese Exclusion Act—the first major step in restricting immigration to the United States.

Meanwhile, Charles Guiteau remained in prison awaiting execution. On June 22, a group of doctors asked President Arthur to postpone the execution while they examined Guiteau's mental condition to determine if he was insane. Attorney General Benjamin Brewster, the government's chief law officer, argued against the delay. The president decided to let the execution go forward. Charles Guiteau was hanged on June 30, 1882.

WHITE HOUSE AND HOME

Arthur continued to veto bills he didn't think should become law. He vetoed the Rivers and Harbors Act, which would have allowed the government to spend about $19 million on improvements to several ports. Arthur argued that the bill benefited only a few parts of the country and not the entire nation. His mysterious adviser, Julia Sand, wrote to him again: "How can I tell you how delighted I was at your veto of the Harbor Bill? Ah, if you only realized what a thrill of enthusiasm you awaken, every time you show the people plainly that you have the good of the whole country at heart."

Congress, however, displayed no such "thrill of enthusiasm." Instead, legislators gathered the votes to override the veto, and the bill became law. Arthur was furious. He vowed to reduce taxes as a way to give part of the government's money back to all citizens.

After Congress adjourned in August, the president returned to New York City. On August 20, he stopped by the home of Julia Sand. This was the first and only time the two met. Julia, he found out, was banker Theodore Sand's daughter, a young unmarried woman with a spinal disability. She and Arthur spent about an hour together, discussing politics.

At about this time, Arthur's doctor visited the White House and noted in his diary that the president was "sick in body and soul." Arthur had developed a kidney disorder called Bright's disease (later called nephritis). Symptoms included nausea, lack of energy, and depression.

Arthur refused to let the public know about his illness, which was then considered fatal. Unaware of the president's physical ailments, one commentator noted in a newspaper editorial: "Mr. Arthur's temperament is sluggish. He is indolent [slow moving]. It requires a great deal of him . . . to begin the dispatch of business. Great questions of public policy bore him."

Chester Arthur kept his presidential hours short and routine. He usually kept Sundays and Mondays to himself. Starting on Tuesday in a typical week, the president arrived at the Oval (presidential) Office about 10:00 A.M. and met with congressmen. At noon on Tuesdays and Fridays, he met with his cabinet in his offices. On Wednesdays, Thursdays, and Saturdays, he met with the members of the public in the White House library. At about 1:00 P.M. he had lunch and then worked for the rest of the afternoon. At 5:00 P.M. he relaxed until dinner, then did no official work after dinner.

The president once told a reporter: "You have no idea how depressing and fatiguing it is to live in the same house where you work." Whenever he could, particularly in the summer, Arthur stayed at the presidential cottage on the grounds of the Soldiers' Home in Washington, D.C. He also loved to fish and took fishing trips as often as he could.

Arthur (left) went fishing whenever he got the chance.

The outside of the White House in the 1880s

✧

The one aspect of his job that Arthur really enjoyed was entertaining. In the fall of 1882, he had the White House completely renovated, at a cost of about $30,000 ($500,000). He had the presidential carriage adorned in leather and lace, with a silver harness for two perfectly matched reddish brown horses. Arthur gave elegant dinners and receptions, with elaborate decorations, magnificent table settings, and the finest of food and wines. He dressed in expensive, custom-tailored clothes and wore tuxedos to dinner. He still liked to stay up until two in the morning, chatting with friends over a good cigar. He sometimes strolled the Washington, D.C., streets afterward, without his customary bodyguard.

The president's son, Alan, also liked fine clothes and elegant parties. He had late-night suppers for college friends at the White House. Arthur tried to shield young Nell from public life. For a time, she lived in the family's New York home

Saint John's Episcopal Church (right) *is only two blocks from the White House.*

——————— ◇

with a governess. In Washington she served as president of the Washington Children's Christmas Club, which gave dinners to poor children.

On Sundays, Arthur sometimes took his children to Saint John's Episcopal Church, near the White House. His wife had sung there in a choir before their marriage. Arthur gave the church a stained-glass window in Ellen's memory and had it set in a place where he could see it from the White House.

CIVIL SERVICE REFORM—AT LAST

In the November 1882 elections, the Democrats gained a majority in both the House and the Senate. But the new Congress was not scheduled to begin until December 3, 1883.

The remaining session of the old Congress, called a lame-duck session, lasted from December 4, 1882, to March 3, 1883. During this time, Republicans and some of their Democratic colleagues worked on major bills. It was a busy ninety days.

In his message to Congress on December 4, 1882, Arthur asked Congress to consider additional reform of the civil service system. He also asked Congress to change tariffs (taxes on goods shipped into the United States from other countries) and to modernize the U.S. Navy. This time Congress listened.

Under the leadership of Democrat George Pendleton, a senator from Ohio, Congress passed the Pendleton Civil Service Reform Act on January 16, 1883. The bill set forth rules for filling some government jobs and required applicants for some jobs to take written tests. It banned kickbacks and established a new commission to manage and oversee the reforms. Most federal workers were not covered under the bill, and tests were required for only a few jobs. But it was a start.

Arthur promptly signed the Pendleton Act into law and worked to make it effective. His support of civil service reform surprised many who remembered how Arthur had given government jobs to his friends when he was part of the New York machine. Some former colleagues from his patronage days in New York were angered and turned against him.

On March 3, 1883—the last day of the session—Congress passed a tariff bill. A special commission had studied how much tariff money the United States collected on goods coming into the country. The commission concluded that tariffs should be reduced by 20 to 25 percent on almost every product. President Arthur agreed, even though influential manufacturers and businessmen in his own party didn't approve of the reduction. To Arthur's great disappointment, the act reduced tariffs an average of less than 2 percent.

That same day, Arthur signed into law a bill to create the Naval War College, a school for naval officers, in

The building of the Naval War College (above) was a cause
Arthur felt strongly about. He signed the bill that created it.

———————————— ◇ ————————————

Newport, Rhode Island, and to build the first steel-hulled
ships for the U.S. Navy. Congress granted funds to build
four new ships—the *Atlanta*, the *Boston*, the *Chicago*, and
the *Dolphin* (called the ABCD ships)—although Arthur had
wanted more. Arthur's secretary of the navy, William
Chandler, was delighted.

"I NEED A HOLIDAY"

Arthur left Washington soon after Congress adjourned. "I
need a holiday as much as the poorest of my fellow citizens," he had once said. But by the end of March, his
health had gotten worse. He decided to take a long vacation in central Florida to regain his strength. The White
House staff announced that the president had a cold.

The train and steamship trip through the South proved
to be exhausting. Arthur suffered miserably. Soon the press

heard that the president appeared very ill. Staff announced that he had had an attack of acute indigestion, but rumors spread. Arthur returned to the White House and immediately announced, "I was never better in my life."

About a month later, on May 24, Arthur joined New York governor Grover Cleveland for the opening of the Brooklyn Bridge. This bridge between Brooklyn and Manhattan in New York was the largest suspension bridge in the world at the time. Afterward, Arthur spent a few days resting in New York.

In late July, the president headed west with some cabinet members and military officers to tour the region around Montana's Yellowstone National Park. On his way, Arthur met chiefs of the Shoshone and Arapaho people, two Native American nations. Along with Interior Secretary Henry Teller, he discussed assistance for Native Americans

———————— ✧ ————————

Arthur was greeted by a group of Shoshone Indians at Fort Washakie, Wyoming Territory, on his way to Yellowstone National Park.

and ways to preserve the western wilderness. Arthur made 350 miles of the trip on horseback. He hiked, fished, and seemed to enjoy himself. But when Arthur got back to Washington in September, he was in great pain and his legs were badly swollen.

Arthur confided in his son and a few others about his disease but refused to tell the public. He continued with

HOUR BY HOUR

Before 1880 people in the United States often set their clocks by looking at the position of the sun in the sky. When the sun was highest, it was "high noon." Because of Earth's rotation, travelers going west or east found that local time varied by about one minute every twelve miles. When railroads spread across the United States, train schedulers and passengers had to deal with more than three hundred different "sun times."

At the suggestion of Connecticut schoolteacher Charles Dowd, the railroads divided the United States into four time zones—eastern, central, mountain, and Pacific—each zone one hour earlier (going west) or later (going east) than the next. The change from sun time to time zones took place on November 18, 1883.

Many Americans criticized the switch to time zones. They accused the railroads of "playing God." They worried that the nation's rural way of life (with people rising with the sun and going to sleep at sunset) was bowing to the demands of industry. But the change to time zones stuck. In November 1884, President Arthur opened the International Meridian Conference, which established time zones for the whole world.

his duties as president throughout the winter and spring of 1884. Still unaware of how ill he was and pleased with his work as president, many people wondered if Arthur would run for a second term.

When the Republican National Convention opened in Chicago on June 4, Arthur allowed his name to be put on the ballot. He did little to promote himself, however. Soon the convention nominated Half-Breed leader James Blaine for president. With nine months left of his presidency, Arthur got back to work.

At a ceremony in Paris on July 4, 1884, France presented the United States with a statue called *Liberty Enlightening the*

——————————— ✧

The head of the Statue of Liberty sits in the Champ de Mars in Paris. The statue was shipped in pieces from France to the United States and then assembled.

World, which became known as the Statue of Liberty. Levi Morton—the U.S. minister to France—represented the president at the ceremony. U.S. laborers laid part of the statue's pedestal in New York Harbor on August 5. The statue itself would arrive in pieces ten months later.

Americans went to the polls on November 4, 1884, and Democrats regained the White House. New York governor Grover Cleveland beat James Blaine in a close race.

CHAPTER NINE

THE FINAL YEARS

I am but one in the 55,000,000; still in the opinion of this one-fifty-five millionth of the country's population, it would be hard indeed to better President Arthur's administration.
—Mark Twain, August 1883

Many people thought Chester Arthur and his cabinet would do little during their last few months in office. Instead, the president continued to push for changes he wanted for the country.

On December 1, 1884—the same day President Arthur delivered his last annual message to Congress— the United States and Nicaragua, a nation in Central America, signed a treaty to build a canal to connect the Atlantic and Pacific oceans. The Frelinghuysen-Zavala Treaty (named for Secretary of State Frelinghuysen and Nicaragua's former president) also included plans for railway and telegraph lines along the canal route.

LINKING THE OCEANS

The proposed canal across Nicaragua, as outlined in the Frelinghuysen-Zavala Treaty, was never built. Instead, the United States completed a canal across Panama, south of Nicaragua, in 1914. The canal allows ships to travel between the Atlantic and the Pacific oceans without making the long journey around the southern tip of South America.

The United States would bear the cost and share ownership with Nicaragua.

In his annual message, Arthur discussed this and other developments in Central and South America. He described treaties and trade agreements. He also reminded Congress of two problem areas: the U.S. economy and the navy. He said that U.S. industries were not operating at their best and that a low level of foreign trade was one of the worst problems facing the United States. The president also reported that the four steel-hulled naval vessels—the ABCD ships—were under construction or launched but that the navy needed to be stronger to face future military threats. "I can not too strongly urge upon [Congress's] attention the duty of restoring our Navy," he said. "[T]he long peace that has lulled us into a sense of fancied security may at any time be disturbed."

WHAT NEXT?

A few days after the president gave his annual message, several Republican leaders met to discuss what Arthur might do next. They urged Arthur to become a candidate for the

U.S. Senate from New York. He turned them down. In January 1885, the soon-to-be former president announced that he would return to his old law firm in New York City.

During his last six weeks in office, President Arthur became more and more ill. Doctors frequently visited the White House. On some days, the president felt stronger. Then he would have a sudden backslide, when he could hardly get out of bed.

On February 22, 1885, Arthur managed to attend the dedication of the cornerstone for the Washington Monument. He read a speech outside on a cold, snowy day and that evening had his last public reception in the White House. About three thousand people attended. To conserve the president's strength in the receiving line, guests filed past in groups of three or four instead of one at a time. Mary McElroy, the president's sister, gave her last reception as the official White House hostess on February 28.

March 4, 1885—Inauguration Day for president-elect Grover Cleveland—was festive and busy. But Arthur was still president until the inauguration ceremony, and Congress remained in session until just before the ceremony began. Arthur had time to sign a bill giving more money to the navy. Congress had also just passed a bill that gave former president Grant a pension (retirement pay). The clock in the Capitol was set back six minutes to give President Arthur time to sign the pension bill into law.

Then Arthur and president-elect Cleveland rode together in a horse-drawn carriage down flag-decorated Pennsylvania Avenue, from the White House to the Capitol. It was a clear, warm day. Thousands of people lined the parade route. The inauguration took place on the east entryway of the Capitol. Between thirty thousand and fifty thousand people watched Cleveland take the oath of office.

Afterward, Arthur gave a luncheon for the new president and watched a fireworks display at the White House. He made sure his belongings were ready for shipment back to New York City and said good-bye to his White House staff. Then he accompanied President Cleveland to the Inaugural Ball that night at the new Pension Building. After the ball, he returned to the Washington home of Secretary of State Frelinghuysen. A few days later, he settled back with his son and daughter in their family home at 123 Lexington Avenue in Manhattan.

A LASTING LEGACY
In May, Frelinghuysen died of hepatitis, and Arthur felt well enough to attend the funeral. Shortly afterward, the former president attended his son's graduation from the College of New Jersey. Alan Arthur then enrolled in Columbia Law School.

When he felt able, Chester Arthur practiced law in an elegant office on the fourth floor of the Mutual Life Building in Manhattan. He did not have a government pension—Congress did not routinely give pensions to U.S. presidents then—but had a salary of $1,000 ($18,000) a month from his law firm. He also earned money from investments and continued to be financially well off. But the effects of Bright's disease often made Arthur's life miserable.

The newspapers finally published the story of Arthur's condition in February 1886. By then the disease had weakened his heart. By March he was critically ill. He drank milk mixed with pepsin (an enzyme that aids digestion) and spent most of his time in bed. His weight fell dramatically. He wrote his will, leaving his property to his children. Two of his sisters—Regina and Mary—came to help care for him.

The warm summer weather brought some improvement in Arthur's health. His family took him to a cottage in New London, Connecticut. But he was too ill to go fishing, which had been one of his favorite activities. He returned to his New York home in the fall and celebrated his fifty-seventh birthday. "I think I'm getting better," he said, "but very slowly."

A few visitors came to see the former president on November 16. One was an old friend, Jimmy Smith, whom Arthur had asked his son to invite over. Alan Arthur watched as Smith filled three large metal garbage cans several times with Arthur's private papers and official documents and then burned the papers.

No one knows exactly why Arthur had Smith do this. But a few months earlier, Arthur had told a former government official that he wished he had done many things differently in his political life. Perhaps he was trying to destroy evidence of his mistakes. Arthur had also told Alan never to go into politics because it had cost him too high a personal price.

The next morning, Arthur's nurse found him unconscious. He had suffered a massive stroke. A newspaper account noted that Arthur later opened his eyes and seemed to recognize those around him. Around midnight the doctor went home while others in the household stayed by Arthur's bedside. Nell, who was then fourteen, was sent off to bed. At 5:10 on the morning of November 18, 1886, Chester Alan Arthur took his last breath.

A green angel stands guard over Arthur's grave at
Albany Rural Cemetery in New York.

Hundreds of people attended Arthur's funeral on November 22 at the Church of the Heavenly Rest. The former president's family was there except for his brother, William, who still held a military job and was stationed in Texas. After the funeral service, Arthur was buried in the family plot at Albany Rural Cemetery. President Cleveland attended the burial.

In 1899 a bronze statue of Chester Arthur was erected on the northeastern corner of New York City's Madison Square Park. On the park's southeastern corner, another statue honors Roscoe Conkling, who froze to death in New York City during the Blizzard of 1888.

Arthur's statue in Madison Square Park was erected thirteen years after his death.

———————— ✧

Ellen Herndon Arthur (the president's Little Nell) married a man named Charles Pinkerton, avoided a public life, and died in 1915 at the age of forty-three. Arthur's letter writer, Julia Sand, continued to be interested in politics, especially civil service reform and tariff issues. She died in 1933, at the age of eighty-three.

Arthur's son—Chester Alan Arthur II—married twice. Deciding not to pursue a career in law after law school, he traveled a lot, invested in real estate, and raised horses. Alan Arthur was once offered the position of U.S. senator from Colorado, but he refused it. He died in 1937, a few days before his seventy-third birthday.

Alan Arthur once said, "I think my father's greatest work was as Quartermaster General of New York State."

In a Lifetime

During the lifetime of Chester A. Arthur (1829–1886), the United States:

- Fought a war with Mexico and a civil war
- Annexed the entire Southwest and West Coast region, from Texas to Washington State
- Built more than 150,000 miles of railroad track
- Grew in population (through childbirth and immigration) from about 12 million people to about 60 million
- Witnessed the invention of the bicycle, the revolver, the stapler, the sewing machine, the typewriter, the machine gun, the safety pin, the lightbulb, the motion picture camera, and Coca-Cola

A railroad crew poses alongside a locomotive in 1885. Railroads grew to crisscross the nation during Arthur's lifetime.

An editorial at the time of Chester Arthur's death offers this view of his presidency: "No duty was neglected in his administration, and no adventurous project alarmed the nation. There was no scandal to make us ashamed. . . . He earned and deserved the honest fame he possesses."

Historians agree that Chester A. Arthur carried out his duties as president honestly and fairly. A biographer, Thomas Reeves, concludes that Arthur did an admirable job, especially considering his ill health, battles with Congress, and the way he became president. Another biographer, Zachary Karabell, sums up his career this way: "In everything he did, Chester Alan Arthur was a gentleman. . . . Arthur managed to be a decent man and a decent president in an era when decency was in short supply. . . . Some people just do the best they can in a difficult situation, and sometimes that turns out just fine."

Although President Arthur burned many of his public and private papers, he saved at least twenty-three letters from Julia Sand. In one letter, she had written: "It is for you to choose whether your record shall be written in black or in gold. For the sake of your country, for our own sake & for the sakes of all who have ever loved you, let it be pure & bright."

When the presidency was unexpectedly forced upon him, Arthur did strive to have his record "written . . . in gold." The major legacy of his administration—and one that Sand was particularly proud of—was the Pendleton Act. It became the foundation for a civil service system that is part of the government of the United States to this day. Although Arthur started his career in machine politics, he ultimately helped lead the nation to a fairer system of government.

Timeline

1829   Chester Alan Arthur is born in North Fairfield, Vermont, on October 5.

1835   The Arthurs move to New York State. Elder Arthur helps start the New York Anti-Slavery Society.

1845   Chester Arthur begins classes at Union College in Schenectady, New York.

1848   Arthur graduates from Union College, begins studying law, and works as a schoolteacher.

1851   Arthur becomes principal of a school in the basement of his father's church in North Pownal, Vermont.

1854   Arthur becomes a lawyer in New York City.

1855   Arthur defends Elizabeth Jennings, an African American who was forced off a streetcar. He works on the Lemmon case, which determines that slaves who travel to New York State are considered free.

1856   Arthur travels to Kansas Territory to support antislavery forces.

1859   Arthur marries Ellen Lewis Herndon on October 25.

1860   William Lewis Herndon Arthur is born on December 10. South Carolina secedes from the Union.

1861   The Civil War begins.

1862   Arthur is named inspector general and then quartermaster general in the New York State militia.

1863   Arthur resigns from the New York State militia on January 1. He returns to his law practice and begins a friendship with influential Republican politician Roscoe Conkling. Arthur's son, William, dies on July 8.

1864 Chester Alan Arthur II is born on July 25.

1871 President Ulysses Grant appoints Arthur to the position of collector at the New York Customhouse. Ellen Herndon Arthur is born on November 21.

1874 Congress bans the moiety system, which allows government officials to make money by seizing illegal imports.

1878 President Rutherford B. Hayes fires Arthur from his customhouse job.

1880 Arthur's wife, Ellen, dies on January 12. Arthur becomes the Republican vice-presidential candidate. He and running mate James Garfield win the election.

1881 Arthur is sworn in as vice president on March 4. President James A. Garfield is shot on July 2 and dies on September 19. Arthur takes the oath of office as president of the United States on September 20 and September 22.

1882 Arthur first vetoes then signs into law the Chinese Exclusion Act, which halts immigration of Chinese laborers for ten years. Arthur learns he has Bright's disease, a kidney disorder.

1883 Arthur signs into law the Pendleton Civil Service Act, which begins to reform the system for hiring federal workers. He also supports and signs legislation to improve the navy and to build steel-hulled naval ships.

1884 Republicans nominate James Blaine as their presidential candidate. He loses the election to Democrat Grover Cleveland on November 4.

1885 Arthur attends the inauguration of President Cleveland on March 4 and later returns to New York City.

1886 The public learns of Arthur's failing health in February. Arthur dies on November 18.

SOURCE NOTES

7 Thomas C. Reeves, *Gentleman Boss: The Life of Chester Alan Arthur* (New York: Alfred A. Knopf, 1975), 245.

8 Kenneth D. Ackerman, *Dark Horse: The Surprise Election and Political Murder of President James A. Garfield* (New York: Carroll and Graf Publishers, 2003), 133.

8 Ibid., 379.

8 Reeves, *Gentleman Boss*, 245.

9 Ibid.

10 Ibid., 12.

10 "Gen. Arthur's Birthplace," *New York Sun*, September 21, 1881, quoted in Reeves, *Gentleman Boss*, 5.

13 "Gen. Arthur at School," *New York Times*, July 28, 1880, quoted in Reeves, *Gentleman Boss*, 8.

16 Reeves, *Gentleman Boss*, 13.

18 Ibid., 14.

20 Ibid., 16.

21 "*Lemmon v. People*, Court of Appeals of New York, 20 NY 562 (March 1860)," http://www.lib.niu.edu/ipo/iht820111.html (October 1, 2004).

24 Reeves, *Gentleman Boss*, 14.

27 Diary of Brodie Herndon, February 26, 1859, Brodie Herndon Papers, University of Virginia, quoted in Reeves, *Gentleman Boss*, 21.

31 Letter from Morgan to U.S. Grant, December 1, 1871, quoted in Reeves, *Gentleman Boss*, 30.

34 Reeves, *Gentleman Boss*, 32.

36 Ibid., 30.

39 Letter to William Arthur Jr., July 9, 1863, quoted in Reeves, *Gentleman Boss*, 35.

40 Reeves, *Gentleman Boss*, 40.

47 Ibid., 51.

48 Mark Twain and Charles Dudley Warner, *The Gilded Age* (Indianapolis: Bobbs-Merrill Company, 1972), 219–20.

51 "The Week," *Nation*, XIII (November 23, 1871), 329, quoted in Reeves, *Gentleman Boss*, 60.

52 Reeves, *Gentleman Boss*, 87.

55 Ibid., 41.

61 "What Thurlow Weed Says," *New York Times*, June 9, 1880, quoted in Reeves, 183.

64 Reeves, *Gentleman Boss*, 180.

65 Ibid., 183.

65 Regina Caw to Alice [Mrs. William] Arthur, June 11, 1880; Arthur family papers, quoted in Reeves, 190.

68 Reeves, *Gentleman Boss*, 221.

71 "Giving Voice to Sorrow," *New York Times*, November 21, 1886, quoted in Reeves, *Gentleman Boss*, 246.

73 Ackerman, *Dark Horse*, 379.

73 Reeves, *Gentleman Boss*, 238.

73 Ackerman, *Dark Horse*, 405.

73 "A Great Nation in Grief," *New York Times*, July 3, 1881, quoted in Reeves, 240.

75 Ackerman, *Dark Horse*, 427.

75 Reeves, *Gentleman Boss*, 247.

76 Ibid., 248–49.

76 Ibid., 254.

79 Reeves, *Gentleman Boss*, 363.

79 Zachary Karabell, *Chester Alan Arthur* (New York: Henry Holt and Company, 2004), 121.

81 Ackerman, *Dark Horse*, 223.

83 "Chester Arthur's 1st Annual Message to Congress—1881," http://www.geocities.com/presidentialspeeches/1881.htm (January 17, 2006).

84 Reeves, *Gentleman Boss*, 279.
85 Letter from Julia Sand to Chester A. Arthur, August 2, 1882, quoted in Reeves, *Gentleman Boss*, 281.
85 Diary of Brodie Herndon, August 1, 1882, quoted in Reeves, *Gentleman Boss*, 318.
85 "Arthur's Policy," *Chicago Tribune*, March 2, 1881, quoted in Reeves, *Gentleman Boss*, 274–75.
86 Karabell, *Chester Alan Arthur*, 94.
90 Reeves, *Gentleman Boss*, 361.
91 Ibid., 359.
95 *Chicago Daily News*, August 3, 1883, quoted in Reeves, *Gentleman Boss*, 369.
96 "Chester Arthur's 4th Annual Message to Congress—1884," http://www.geocities.com/presidentialspeeches/1884.htm (January 17, 2006).
99 Reeves, *Gentleman Boss*, 417.
101 Vernon B. Hampton interview with Chester A. Arthur II, December 5, 1931, Hampton Papers, quoted in Reeves, *Gentleman Boss*, 31.
103 "Ex-President Arthur," Editorial, *New York World*, November 20, 1886, quoted in Reeves, Gentleman Boss, 423–24.
103 Karabell, *Chester Alan Arthur*, 143.
103 Reeves, *Gentleman Boss*, 246.

Selected Bibliography

Ackerman, Kenneth D. *Dark Horse: The Surprise Election and Political Murder of President James A. Garfield*. New York: Carroll & Graf Publishers, 2003.

Holland, Barbara. *Hail to the Chiefs: How to Tell Your Polks from Your Tylers*. New York: Ballantine Books, 1990.

Karabell, Zachary. *Chester Alan Arthur*. New York: Henry Holt and Company, 2004.

Kunhardt, Philip, Jr., et al. *The American President*. New York: Riverhead Books, 1999.

Reeves, Thomas C. *Gentleman Boss: The Life of Chester Alan Arthur*. New York: Alfred A. Knopf, 1975.

Summers, Mark Wahlgren. *Rum, Romanism & Rebellion: The Making of a President, 1884*. Chapel Hill: University of North Carolina Press, 2000.

Whitney, David C. *The American Presidents*. 8th ed. Pleasantville, NY: Reader's Digest Association, Inc., 1993.

Further Reading and Websites

Albany Rural Cemetery
http://www.albanyruralcemetery.org/
Visitors to this site can take a virtual tour of the cemetery in which Chester Arthur and his family are buried. The site contains information about the monument to President Arthur there.

Arnold, James R. *The Civil War*. Minneapolis: Twenty-First Century Books, 2005.

Brunelli, Carol. *Chester A. Arthur: Our Twenty-first President*. Chanhassen, MN: The Child's World, 2002.

DuTemple, Lesley A. *The New York Subways*. Minneapolis: Twenty-First Century Books, 2003.

Elish, Dan. *Chester A. Arthur*. Danbury, CT: Children's Press, 2004.

Feldman, Ruth Tenzer. *James Garfield*. Minneapolis: Twenty-First Century Books, 2005.

Gelman, Amy. *New York*. Minneapolis: Lerner Publications Company, 2002.

Goldman, David J. *Presidential Losers*. Minneapolis: Millbrook Press, 2004.

Greene, Meg. *Into the Land of Freedom*. Minneapolis: Twenty-First Century Books, 2004.

Hakim, Joy. *Reconstructing America*. 3rd ed. New York: Oxford University Press, 2003.

Havelin, Kate. *Ulysses S. Grant*. Minneapolis: Twenty-First Century Books, 2005.

Homberger, Eric. *Mrs. Astor's New York: Money and Social Power in a Gilded Age*. New Haven, CT: Yale University Press, 2002.

Kendall, Martha E. *Failure Is Impossible*. Minneapolis: Twenty-First Century Books, 2001.

Levy, Debbie. *Rutherford B. Hayes*. Minneapolis: Twenty-First Century Books, 2007.

Our Documents
http://www.ourdocuments.gov
This site contains one hundred milestone documents in U.S. history, including several that relate specifically to the work of Chester A. Arthur. These documents include the Kansas-Nebraska Act, the Emancipation Proclamation, the Chinese Exclusion Act, and the Pendleton Act.

Sonneborn, Liz. *The Shoshones*. Minneapolis: Lerner Publications Company, 2007.

Index

ABOUT THE AUTHOR

Ruth Tenzer Feldman has written biographies and history books for children, including *Don't Whistle in School* and *How Congress Works*. She grew up in Long Branch, New Jersey, not far from where President Garfield died, and—as a legislative attorney for the U.S. Department of Education—she was part of the civil service President Arthur helped to create.

Ruth lives in Portland, Oregon, with her husband, corgi, and trusty computer. There's a lot more about her at www.ruthtenzerfeldman.com, where you can contact her. She would enjoy hearing from you.

———————— ✧ ————————